W9-AJS-999

# HOBBY AND COMPETITION
# ROBOTS

## BY GEORGE ANTHONY KULZ

**CONTENT CONSULTANT**
Tariq Tashtoush
Assistant Professor of Engineering
Texas A&M International University

**Core Library**

An Imprint of Abdo Publishing
abdopublishing.com

Cover image: The combat robot Kuratas stands on
exhibit at a museum in Tokyo.

**abdopublishing.com**

Published by Abdo Publishing, a division of ABDO, PO Box 398166, Minneapolis, Minnesota 55439. Copyright © 2019 by Abdo Consulting Group, Inc. International copyrights reserved in all countries. No part of this book may be reproduced in any form without written permission from the publisher. Core Library™ is a trademark and logo of Abdo Publishing.

Printed in the United States of America, North Mankato, Minnesota
042018
092018

Cover Photo: Yoshikazu Tsuno/AFP/Getty Images
Interior Photos: Yoshikazu Tsuno/AFP/Getty Images, 1; Mustafa Yalcin/Anadolu Agency/Getty Images, 4–5; Adam Gray/Barcroft Media/Getty Images, 7; Doug Strickland/Chattanooga Times Free Press/AP Images, 9; Dan Materna/AFP/Getty Images, 12–13, 43; Red Line Editorial, 15; Rick Rycroft/AP Images, 20–21; Drone Photography/Shutterstock Images, 24, 33; Joerg Mitter/Red Bull/AP Images, 26; George Rizer/Boston Globe/Getty Images, 28–29, 45; Rod Aydelotte/Waco Tribune-Herald/AP Images, 34; MegaBots/Cover Images/Newscom, 36–37

Editor: Bradley Cole
Imprint Designer: Maggie Villaume
Series Design Direction: Ryan Gale

**Library of Congress Control Number: 2017962827**

**Publisher's Cataloging-in-Publication Data**

Names: Kulz, George Anthony, author.
Title: Hobby and competition robots / by George Anthony Kulz.
Description: Minneapolis, Minnesota : Abdo Publishing, 2019. | Series: Robot innovations | Includes online resources and index.
Identifiers: ISBN 9781532114670 (lib.bdg.) | ISBN 9781532154508 (ebook)
Subjects: LCSH: Personal robotics--Juvenile literature. | Mechanical engineering--Juvenile literature. | Combat--Juvenile literature. | Robots--Juvenile literature.
Classification: DDC 796.15--dc23

# CONTENTS

# CHAPTER ONE

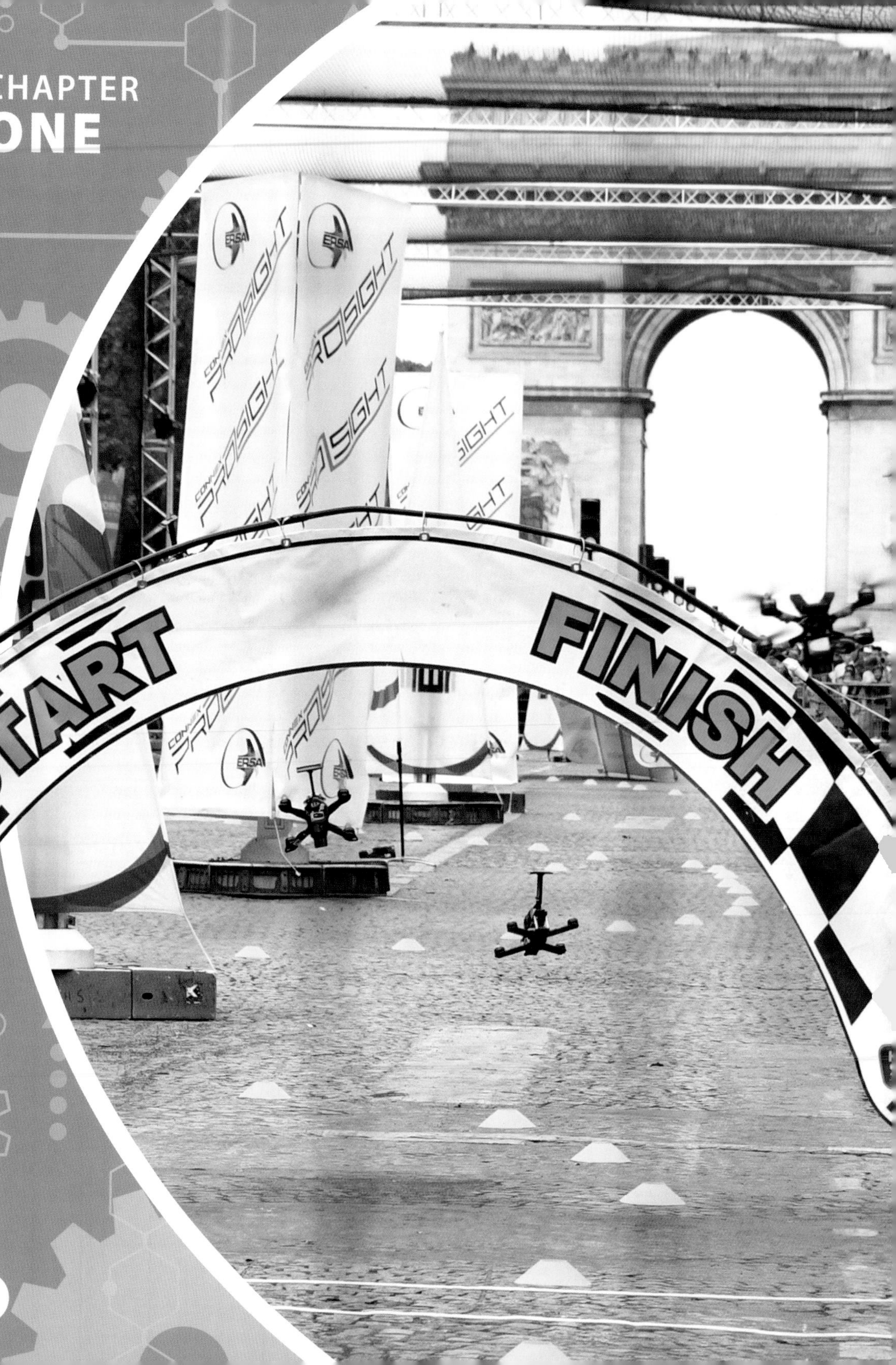

# WHAT ARE HOBBY AND COMPETITION ROBOTS?

The pilot of the green drone dives under the starting gate. He speeds along, racing behind another aircraft. The orange drone in front of him flies low. He follows and attempts to overtake it. The orange drone hugs the turn. The green drone is unable to pass. The two exit the turn and do a quick turn to the right to enter the next one.

That's when the orange drone bangs into a wall. The copter spins crazily. It crashes, sending pieces flying.

Drones fly under a starting gate to start another lap at a drone race.

## INSIDE RACING DRONES

A lot of parts go into racing drones. First, there's a radio-control system. It includes a computer, motor, antenna, and propellers. The antenna receives signals from a control box. The computer figures out the command from the box. It then tells the motor how to turn the propellers to move the drone. Second, there's a first-person viewing (FPV) system. A camera is mounted on the drone. A headset transmits what the camera sees. Finally, it needs a power source. A small, powerful battery provides electricity to the drone's systems.

The green drone speeds across the finish line. The pilot takes off his virtual reality goggles and jumps up and down. He has just won his first Drone Racing League (DRL) drone race. This is the world of hobby and competition robots.

## THE DRONE RACING LEAGUE

In 2015, Nicholas Horbaczewski saw his first drone race. People have been flying

Nicholas Horbaczewski shows off a drone to promote the Drone Racing League he founded.

# DESIGNING ROBOTS

## THE DRONES AND RACE COURSES OF THE DRL

The DRL builds the drones used for each race. Drones in DRL races travel approximately 80 miles per hour (130 km/h). The drones are all built the same. This means that no drone has an advantage. The pilots must rely on their flying skills to win.

The DRL also builds its own courses. Courses are made up of LED hoops and obstacles. They are built in abandoned buildings and stadiums around the world. During the DRL's first international championships in 2017, the course was constructed in a London palace that was originally built in 1873.

remote-controlled aircraft for decades. However, these aircraft were different. Pilots wore first-person viewing (FPV) headsets, allowing them to see from a camera mounted on the drone's body. It was like being inside the drone as it flew.

Horbaczewski wanted to organize a drone racing sport. Pilots would race in different courses around the world. Viewers could watch the races on TV or the

High school students make repairs to their robot during an exhibition.

internet like other sporting events. He came up with the Drone Racing League.

The first series of DRL events was held in 2016. The events attracted 28 million viewers. In 2017, that number grew to 75 million for this fast-growing sport.

## WHAT ARE HOBBY AND COMPETITION ROBOTS?

Robots are an important part of society. They work in factories and hospitals. Robots help humans solve problems. They make great toys. They even work in space. Robots for these tasks have to be built just right.

Some people enjoy tinkering with robots. They design and build robots as a hobby. These hobbyists learn about electronics and computer programming. Some make robots to do simple tasks around the house, such as opening doors and answering phones. Others make robots that will compete in races or battles. The uses for hobby robots are limited only by the builder's imagination.

Drone racing is only one type of competition. Robots play soccer against each other, fight each other, and perform timed tasks. For hobbyists, competitions are a way to show what they've done. They're also a way to get together with other hobbyists, exchange ideas, and have fun.

# STRAIGHT TO THE
# SOURCE

Horbaczewski talks about the people who race drones in the Drone Racing League:

> All different physical types and ability levels can get into drone racing. We have pilots who are stockbrokers, and we have pilots who unload trucks at Macy's. And that gets me really excited, because I think it creates aspirational sports figures for a really wide and diverse set of people. We get to be athletes and nerds and scientists all in the same day.
>
> Source: Kara Weisenstein. "Is Drone Racing the High-Speed Sport of the Future?" *Creators.* VICE Media LLC, February 3, 2016. Web. February 6, 2018.

## Back It Up

Horbaczewski is using evidence to support a point. Write a paragraph describing the point he is making. Then write down two or three pieces of evidence Horbaczewski uses to make the point.

# CHAPTER TWO

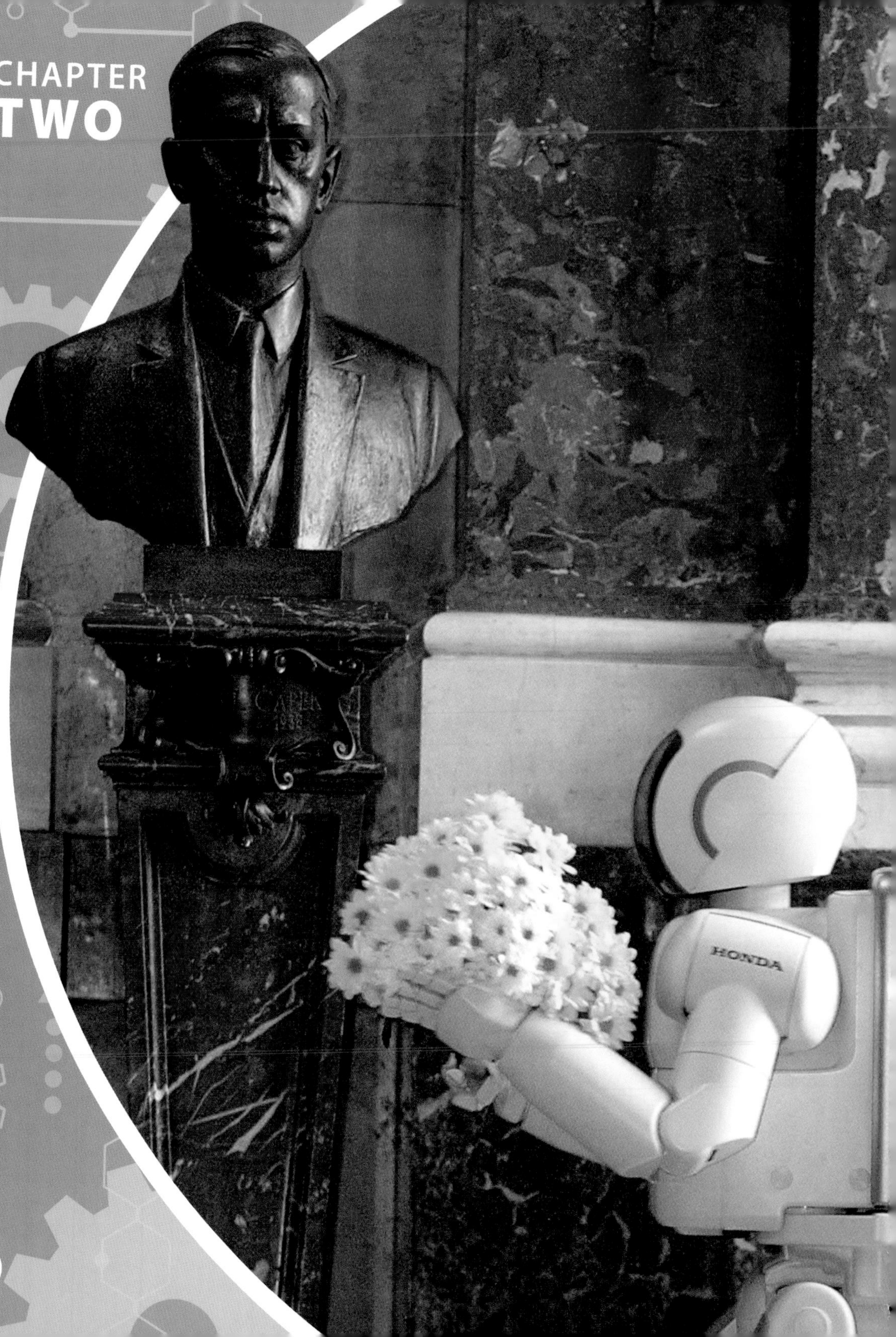

# ADVANCES IN ROBOT TECHNOLOGY

The word *robot* was first used in a play written in 1920 by Karel Čapek. It came from the Czech word *robota*, which means "forced labor." In the play, the robots were built to be slaves. Today, the word *robot* is used to describe something that is built to perform a particular task that humans usually do.

The first automaton was built around 400 BCE. Automatons are machines that follow predetermined actions. Archytas, a Greek mathematician, made a wooden bird that could move on its own. He attached the bird to a bar

The Honda Asimo robot brings flowers to a bust of Karel Čapek.

that moved in a circle. Then he applied steam or air to it. The air pushed the bird so that it appeared to fly.

## COMPUTERS AND ARTIFICIAL INTELLIGENCE

Today, most robots are controlled by computers and appear to have minds of their own. In 1954, George Devol created Unimate. It was the first computer-controlled robot. It was an arm that was used in factories. Although Unimate was not a hobby robot, George Devol's ideas were very important to hobbyists.

In 1969, Shakey became the first robot with artificial intelligence (AI). It was built by SRI International. AI is the ability of a robot to think. Shakey was given tasks to do. It did them all by itself with no help from people.

## THE FIRST COMPETITION ROBOTS

In 1970, engineering professor Woodie Flowers was a teaching assistant in the Introduction to Design and Manufacturing course at the Massachusetts Institute of Technology (MIT). Students were given a box of parts.

# IMPORTANT
# MILESTONES

There have been some amazing discoveries related to hobby and competition robots. What do you notice about the progress from the first robots to today? What progress has there been in what they can do and how they are built? Where do you think the hobby will be in 50 years?

**400 BCE:** Archytas builds a steam-powered bird.

**1920:** Karel Čapek's play about robots debuts.

**1954:** George Devol builds Unimate, the first computer-controlled robot.

**1969:** RI International builds Shakey, the first robot with AI.

**1970:** MIT starts its Introduction to Design course and robot competition.

**1988:** MileHiCon hosts the first Critter Crawl.

**1989:** Denver Mad Scientists Club holds the first Critter Crunch.

**1992:** The group For Inspirations and Recognition of Science Technology (FIRST) has its first robot competition.

**1994:** Marc Thorpe holds his first Robot Wars.

**1997:** The first all-robot soccer game is held.

**2005:** The Arduino computer first becomes available.

**2016:** The first Drone Racing League race is held.

**2017:** The first giant robot duel is held.

They used the parts to build machines to do a task. They competed to see whose machine could complete the task the fastest. This was the first robot contest.

In 1988, the first Critter Crawl was held in Denver, Colorado, at a science fiction convention called MileHiCon. Creators presented electronic and wind-up toys to an audience. The "critters" were judged based on speed, creativity, and design. The following year, the Denver Mad Scientists Club held one of the first robot wars at MileHiCon. They called it the Critter Crunch. Small robots, weighing 20 pounds (9 kg) or less, battled on a tabletop until there was one left standing.

## ROBOT WARS

Robot Wars is a robot competition started in 1994 by Marc Thorpe. He got the idea from two failed business ideas. One idea was a line of toy vehicles that would fight with weapons. The other was a remote-controlled vacuum cleaner.

Then he thought about combining the two ideas. He pictured robots with weapons that fought in an arena. He came up with the idea for the first Robot Wars. Robot Wars had three events. The first was a one-on-one fight between each robot. In the second event each robot guided another robot across a finish line. A "house" robot would try to stop it. Finally, the last event involved a death match with all the robots. The last robot standing would be the winner.

# NON-FIGHTING ROBOTS

Although robot battles are very popular, there are many non-fighting robot competitions. One competition is called the Amazing MicroMouse Contest. In 1997, Donald Christiansen, editor of *Spectrum* magazine, challenged readers to design robotic mice that could find their way through a maze. Five mice competed in the first race. By 2014, there were more than 100 contests globally.

Another competition involves robots playing soccer. Robot soccer came

## DESIGNING ROBOTS

### THE FIRST ROBOT WARS WINNER

The winner of the first Robot Wars competition in 1994 was Charles Tilford, an inventor. His robot was the South Bay Mauler. It was made from an old washtub. He connected two maces to the tub with chains. A gear motor spun the maces in circles.

The South Bay Mauler lost its one-on-one battle. Its battery was knocked out, and it stopped moving. However, the South Bay Mauler was the last robot standing during the final battle.

from scientists in Japan researching robots and AI. They wanted to use soccer to test ideas about robot movement, learning, and cooperation. The first RoboCup games were held in 1996. By the following year, more than 40 teams competed, and 5,000 people watched the games. RoboCup soccer is still popular in the 2010s.

## EXPLORE ONLINE

Chapter Two talks about Woodie Flowers and his Introduction to Design and Manufacturing course at MIT. The article at the website below goes into more depth on Woodie Flowers. What information does the website give about Woodie Flowers and his ideas about competition robots? How is the information from the website the same as the information in Chapter Two? What new information did you learn from the website?

### WOODIE FLOWERS, A PIONEER OF HANDS-ON ENGINEERING EDUCATION
abdocorelibrary.com/hobby-robots

# CHAPTER THREE

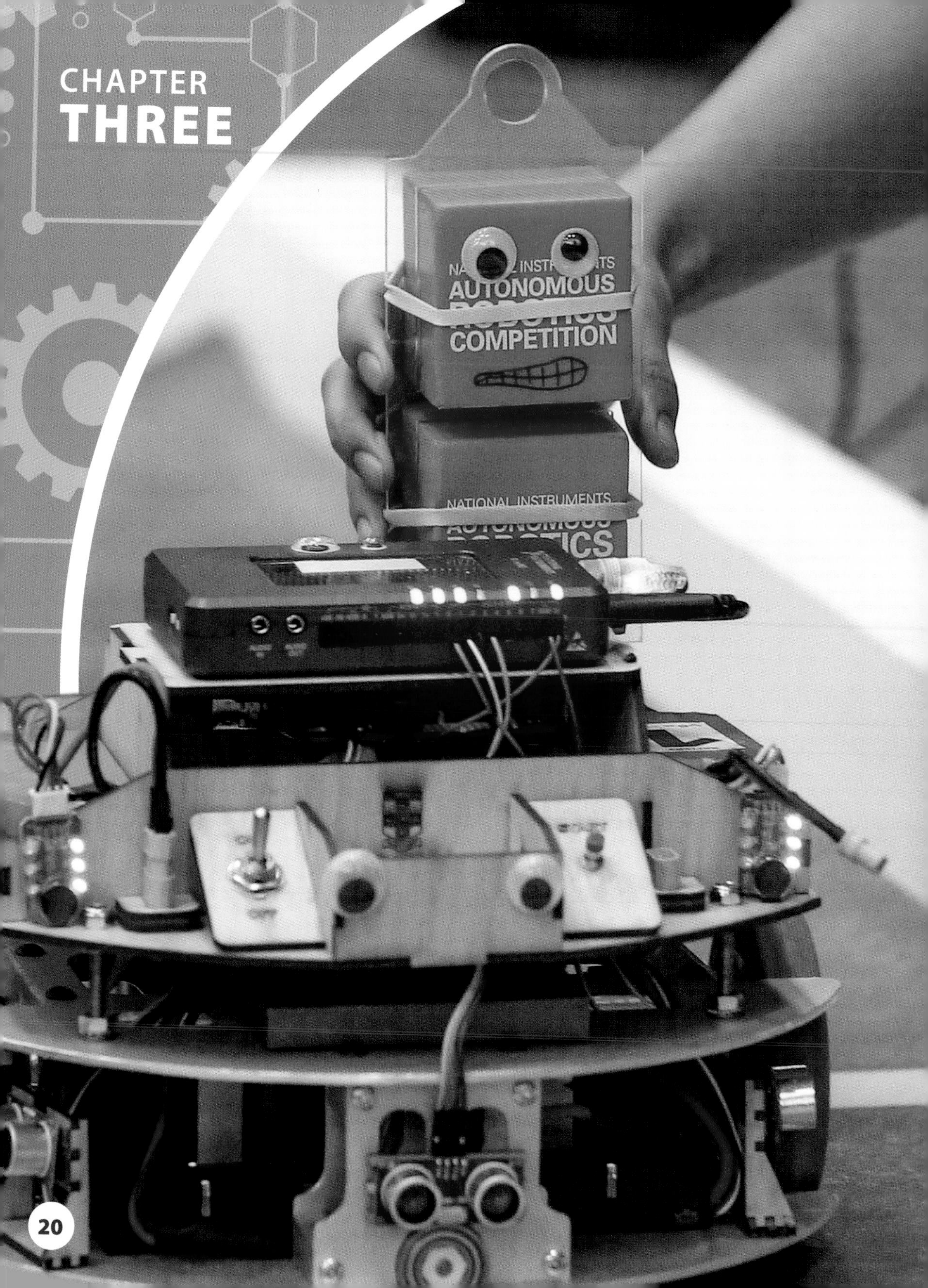

# CHALLENGES OF BUILDING ROBOTS

**B**uilding hobby and competition robots can be fun. It also can be challenging. Robot designers must choose the best way to power their robots. They also must find the best materials to use. Competition robots must be built well to have a chance of winning. They need to respond to a remote controller or be able to make decisions on their own. Finally, hobby and competition robot builders must make sure their robots are safe around people and property.

Design often focuses on how to achieve a task or goal rather than how the robot looks.

# POWER

All robots need power to make them work. There are two types of power for hobby and competition robots. Alternating current (AC) is electricity from outlets in a house. AC-powered robots need to stay plugged in. Direct current (DC) is power that comes from a battery. Most hobby and competition robots, like drones, need DC power to move long distances. Drone propellers need lots of power. Strong batteries are needed to power them. The stronger the battery, the heavier it is. The heavier the battery, the more the robot will weigh. The more a robot weighs, the more power it will need. Heavy robots use a lot of power and generally are not able to travel far.

# MATERIALS

Materials for a hobby or competition robot depend on what it will be doing. Common materials to use are wood, plastic, metal, and carbon composites. Wood and plastic are cheaper and easier to use than metal or carbon composites. They are also very light. However, they are not very durable. Metal and carbon composites are much more durable than wood or plastic. They are better for battle robots. They are also good for outdoor robots like drones. However, they are more expensive, harder to use, and can be heavy. They are more expensive to replace when they become damaged in battle or in crashes.

## CHEAPER WAYS TO BUILD HOBBY ROBOTS

Starting with robot kits may be better than building a robot from scratch. Kits are cheaper than buying individual parts. Robot kits include a complete set of robot parts. They also include software to program the robot. Builders can build different robots from one set of parts.

3-D printers are another way to build robots cheaply. These printers stack layers of material to build three-dimensional parts. 3-D printers can use materials like resin, plastics, and steel, to make parts. A 3-D printer can make propellers or special joints. Instructions on how to build each part are sent from a computer to the printer.

Drones are often made of carbon fiber and plastic to reduce weight and increase strength.

## RESPONSIVENESS

Another challenge is getting a robot to respond to controls. For example, drones need to respond quickly to a remote controller when racing. Most robots have a receiver which listens to signals from the remote control. They also have a small computer that functions like a brain. The brain controls motors, displays, and cameras. The receiver listens to commands from the remote control. The brain takes the commands and changes them to signals to control the propeller motors.

Remote controls and hobby robots use radio frequencies to communicate. Lower frequencies travel far. However, when racing FPV drones, ultra-high frequencies need to be used. These frequencies are needed to send information from the drone's camera. This limits how far the drone can go from the controller.

## DESIGNING ROBOTS

### THE MIGHTY ARDUINO

One of the most popular robot brains is the Arduino. It was created in 2005 by Massimo Banzi. The Arduino is a computer on a circuit board smaller than a deck of cards. It has plenty of connectors to plug into motors, displays, lights, and even other computers. Banzi was frustrated by existing computers. They were expensive and didn't have the power he wanted. The Arduino is easy to build and use on lots of different robots. Plus, it starts at just $20.

# SAFETY

One of the biggest challenges is letting hobby and competition robots loose in the real world. Robots are made of hard parts. These parts can injure people and property if they get too close. Robot battles must be held in special areas away from people. This is so robots don't come in contact with people accidentally.

Drones need to follow special rules. Because they are like planes, they have to follow Federal Aviation Authority (FAA) rules that apply to planes. Because they also use radio frequencies, they have to follow Federal Communications Commission (FCC) radio frequency rules.

Crowds stand behind nets during a Drone Racing League event to stay out of harm's way.

# CHAPTER FOUR

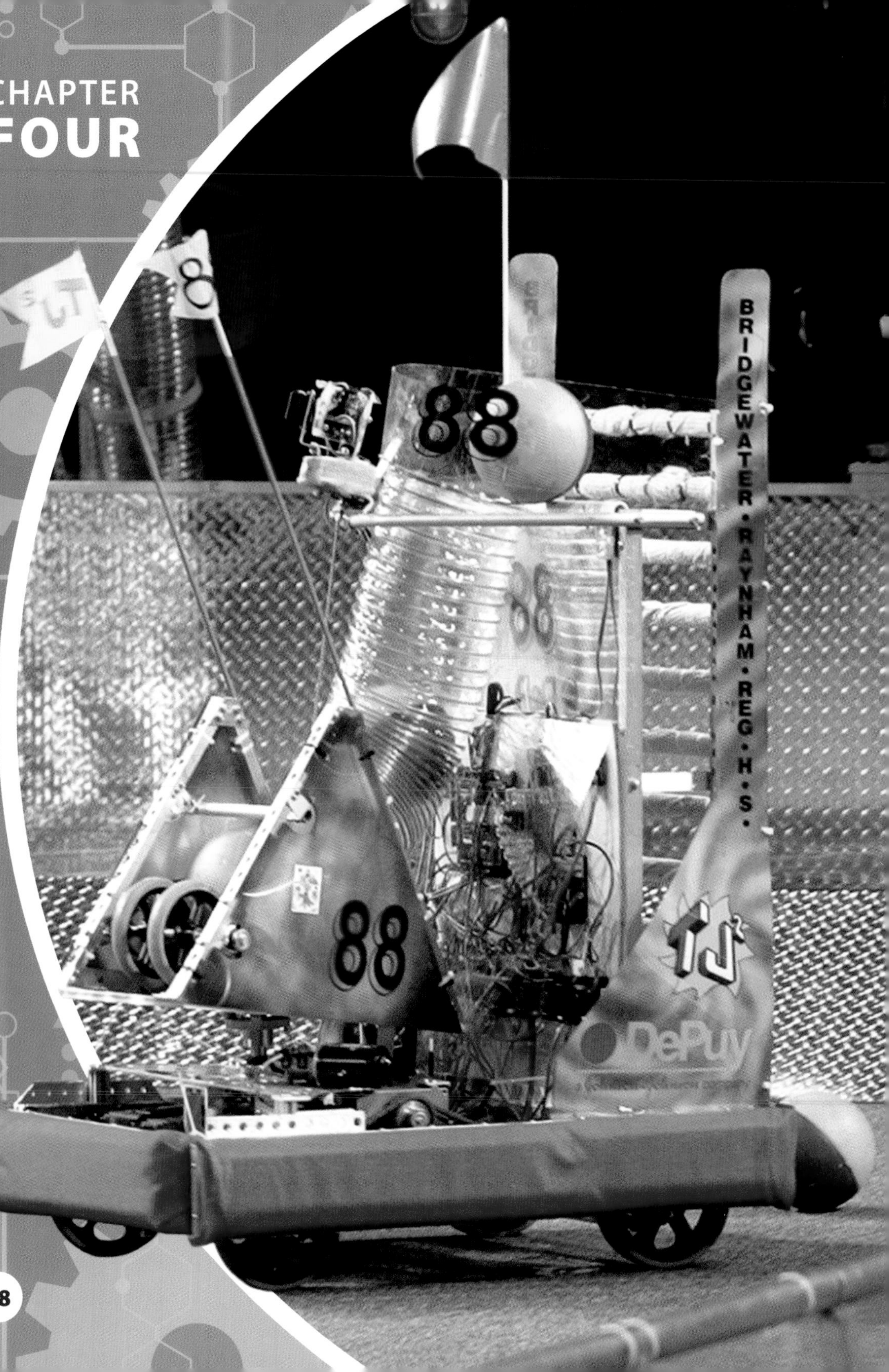

# ROBOTS IN ACTION

Many people find building robots exciting. In schools, classes and clubs allow students to learn about building robots. People build robots in their garages or basements. Many people enjoy watching robot competitions. Hobby and competition robots spark the imaginations of people around the world.

## ROBOT WARS ON TV

The original Robot Wars was started in 1994. In 1998, *Robot Wars* became a popular TV show in the United Kingdom. By 2016, two million people were watching *Robot Wars*. Today, the TV show looks very different from the original

Robotics competitions teach students many valuable skills.

## NOT JUST ABOUT ROBOTICS

Dean Kamen came up with a competition called For Inspirations and Recognition of Science Technology (FIRST). It brings MIT's design class to younger children. Woodie Flowers from MIT is an adviser for the FIRST programs. Their first competition was held in 1992.

In 2017, an all-girl team from Afghanistan won the contest in Europe. The task involved cleaning water. It also involved bringing water from place to place. FIRST is not just about robots. Kids solve real-world problems and work with other kids from around the globe.

Robot Wars. It focuses on the robot battles. Robots compete in groups. Winners progress to the next round. The winners of each group fight in a final battle. During the final battle, the robots avoid obstacles and the house robots.

## ROBOT SOCCER

Robot soccer is another event that is popular today. RoboCup has a number of leagues. Robot players can be from 6 inches (15 cm) tall to approximately 50 to 70 inches (1.2 to 1.8 m) tall. The Humanoid and

Standard Platform leagues have human-looking players. The Standard Platform League's robots all look the same. The Mid Size league has robots that look like traffic cones. Finally, the Small Size league has small, flat robots that look like Roombas. This is the only league where robot teams are controlled by a single computer. In the other leagues, individual robots move and figure things out on their own.

## DESIGNING ROBOTS

### DESIGNING A WINNING *ROBOT WARS* ROBOT

In 2017, father-and-son team Adrian and Michael Oates won the tenth season of *Robot Wars*. Their winning robot, Eruption, competed in seasons 8 and 9 as well but never won a trophy. Eruption is a flipper robot. It wedges itself under other robots and flips them over. It also has interchangeable weapons. It has a blade that can slice through other robots and a claw. The robot's armor is extra strong to protect from other robots' blades. In its final battle with a robot called Carbide, Eruption didn't defeat Carbide. However, the judges ruled that Eruption fought the best.

# SWORD COMPETITIONS BETWEEN HUMAN AND ROBOT

Some competition robots are not hobby robots. The MOTOMAN-MH24 is an industrial robotic arm. It was built by Yaskawa Electric Corporation. Industrial robots work in factories. Yaskawa Electric Corporation wanted to show how accurate its robot was. The company held a contest between the robot and Isao Machii, a Japanese sword master.

First, Yaskawa recorded Machii's movements. They used those movements to program the robot. It took three months for the robot to learn the movements. For the contest, the robot and Machii each had to slice through fruit and rolled-up straw mats. The robot was not as fast as Machii. However, the robot could do everything Machii could do.

## DRONE RACING

Drone racing is a popular sport for hobbyists. FPV racing is the more common version of this sport. Non-FPV

# PARTS OF A DRONE
# RACER

In this diagram, important parts of a racing drone are labeled. Think of another competition robot you've read about in Chapter Four. Find a picture of it. Try to label the parts of the robot. What do you think each part does?

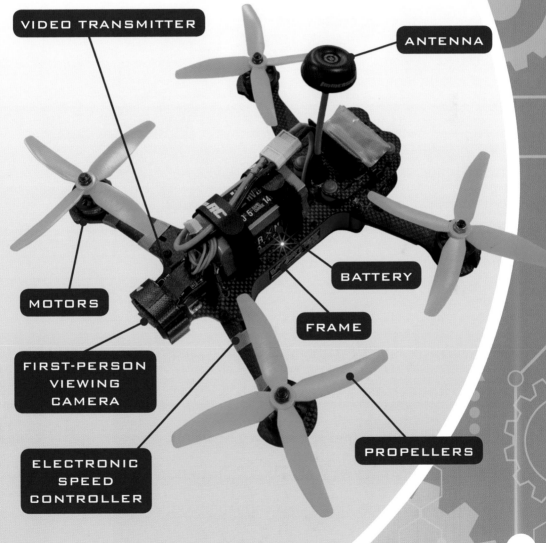

VIDEO TRANSMITTER

ANTENNA

MOTORS

BATTERY

FRAME

FIRST-PERSON VIEWING CAMERA

ELECTRONIC SPEED CONTROLLER

PROPELLERS

High school students prepare their robot for a competition at their school.

racing is also still popular. The Drone Racing League is just one drone racing organization. Others include International Drone Racing Association (IDRA) and Rotorcross.

Drone racing is not just about flying. There are robot boat races as well. The organization Microtransat holds boat races that cross the Atlantic Ocean.

# ROBOTS AT HOME

There are many amazing hobby robots that are built for fun. In 2013, two girls built a small-scale model of the Mars rover *Spirit*. Camille and Genevieve Beatty were 13 and 11 years old at the time. *Spirit* was sent to Mars in 2003. It explored the surface and took lots of pictures. The girls' robot is solar-powered. It has sensors to look for heat and light sources. It uses sonar to find its way around. It was displayed at the New York Hall of Science in New York City in 2013.

## FURTHER EVIDENCE

Chapter Four covers hobby and competition robots in action. What was one of the main points of this chapter? What evidence is included to support this point? Read the article at the website below. Does the information on the website support the main point of the chapter? Does it present new evidence?

### THE ROBOT ART COMPETITION
abdocorelibrary.com/hobby-robots

# CHAPTER
# FIVE

# THE FUTURE OF ROBOTICS

Robots have come a long way from automatons. Hobbyists are always improving their robots. They are also finding new cool and useful things to do with them.

## GIANT ROBOT LEAGUE

In 2014, Gui Cavalcanti and Matt Oehrlein started a company called MegaBots. They loved movies, video games, and comic books with giant fighting robots. Their goal was to have yearly robot battles. They sent a challenge to a Japanese

Eagle Prime was built by MegaBots and has fought in a giant robot duel.

robotics team, Suidobashi Heavy Industries. In 2017, the two teams' robots met head-to-head.

The American robot, Eagle Prime, was 16 feet (4.8 m) tall and weighed 12 tons (10.8 metric tons). The Japanese robot, Kuratas, was 13 feet (4 m) tall and weighed 6.5 tons (5.8 metric tons). They both had human-shaped heads and bodies. They were both driven by pilots riding inside the robots' body. Eagle Prime moved using tank treads. Kuratas moved on three wheels. Both were equipped with paint guns and weapons. During the battle, Eagle Prime prevented Kuratas from moving by pushing against it. After getting stuck together, Eagle Prime used a chainsaw. Bits of Kuratas's arm were damaged. Eagle Prime was declared the winner.

## ROBOCUP 2050

Robots play soccer against each other. The goal is to have a robotic team ready by 2050. Supporters of the RoboCup suggest that the human winners of the 2050 World Cup would play an all-robot team. The technology doesn't exist yet to do this. By setting small, reachable goals along the way, they are confident they will make this happen.

## WHAT DOES THE FUTURE HOLD?

## SOCCER-PLAYING ROBOTS

The key to meeting the RoboCup 2050 goal is AI. Robots need to act like people. Real players know rules and strategies. They communicate with other players. They adapt to what's around them. They can be forceful or cautious. They make decisions. With AI, robots can use information to appear to have personality. All these qualities may make them appear human.

As technology improves, building hobby robots is becoming easier. 3-D printers allow anyone to create robot parts. Telling robots what to do is also getting easier. Robots will be smarter. AI will allow hobby robots to think. Soon robots will make their own decisions. The ultimate goal of AI is to make a robot act just like a person. Humans learn by reading information. They can talk to one another.

## DESIGNING ROBOTS

### 3-D PRINTED DRONE BATTERIES

In 2013, Jennifer A. Lewis, a professor at Harvard University, made the first miniature battery using a 3-D printer. The battery was the size of a grain of sand. The printer used materials that conduct electricity. One of the battery's potential uses is to power a miniature drone. 3-D printers are becoming more common. Someday, hobbyists may be able to create their own small, lightweight batteries for their drones.

They can sense the world around them. AI hobby robots may be able to do all these things someday.

People building hobby and competition robots make advances that are useful in other fields. RoboCup also holds rescue and home competitions. In RoboCup Rescue, robots work in a hazardous environment looking for people that need rescuing. RoboCup@Home robots compete in tasks that help people at home. Hobbyists are not only building robots for themselves. They're also building them to solve the problems of the future.

# STRAIGHT TO THE
# SOURCE

Jack Langelaan talks about how racing drone technology can be used in other areas of society. He said:

> Situation awareness is a key problem in drone operations. . . . Vision systems consisting of several cameras and a computer to stitch together the different views could help, or a [touch sensitive] system could vibrate to alert a pilot to the presence of a drone or other obstacle nearby. Those sorts of technologies to improve the pilot's awareness during a race could also be used to assist a remote-control robot pilot operating a vehicle at an oil drilling platform or near a hydrothermal vent in the deep ocean.

> Source: Jack Langelaan. "How Might Drone Racing Drive Innovation?" *The Conversation*. The Conversation, June 10, 2016. Web. February 6, 2018.

## Changing Minds

This text discusses an opinion that hobby robotics is important to the future. Take a position on this, then imagine that your best friend has the opposite opinion. Write a short essay trying to change your friend's mind. Make sure you detail your opinion and your reasons for it. Include facts and details that support your reasons.

# FAST FACTS

- Hobby robots are robots that are built for fun and are not meant to be sold or used in industry.

- Competition robots are robots that compete against each other to perform a task.

- The first robot competition was held in 1970. It was part of MIT's Introduction to Design course.

- Hobby robot builders are faced with challenges related to power, materials, and the responsiveness of their robots.

- Robots have to follow a lot of strict rules in society. Robots also have to be aware of the safety of the people around them.

- There are many kinds of robot competitions. Some play soccer, some fight each other, and some race.

- The FIRST organization brings robot programs and competitions to kids in elementary through high school all over the world.

- Today, robot competitions mostly involve robots. Someday in the future, robots and people might compete against each other more regularly.

43

# STOP AND
# THINK

### Another View

This book talks about one of the first computer-controlled robots, Unimate. Some say it was the first of its kind, while others do not. Ask a librarian or another adult to help you find sources about the first computer-controlled robot. Write a short essay comparing and contrasting the sources' points of view. What is the point of view of each author? How are they similar and why? How are they different and why?

### You Are There

This book discusses the first Robot Wars. Imagine you are there when the robots battle. Write a letter home telling your friends what you have seen. What do you notice about the robots? Be sure to add plenty of details to your notes.

### Dig Deeper

After reading this book, what questions do you still have about hobby and competition robots? With an adult's help, find a few reliable sources that can help you answer your questions. Write a paragraph about what you learned.

## Take a Stand

The RoboCup 2050 supporters want to have an all-robot soccer team play an all-human soccer team by the year 2050. Currently, robot teams play against other robot teams. Do you think it's worth building an all-robot soccer team? Do you think it's a good idea that robots play against people? Or should soccer be for only people to play? Why?

# GLOSSARY

**antenna**
a device used to send or receive radio signals

**artificial intelligence (AI)**
the ability of a robot to think like a person can

**composites**
materials that are made up of more than one different type of material

**current**
the flow of electricity through something

**drone**
an unmanned aerial vehicle, usually operated by remote control

**industrial**
related to businesses that make things

**motor**
a machine that causes something mechanical to move

**remote controller**
a device that sends radio signals to another device to tell it what to do

**sonar**
a method used to find things by sending sound waves and measuring the time it takes them to bounce back

**3-D printers**
printers that create 3-D objects by building them in layers with material

# ONLINE RESOURCES

To learn more about hobby and competition robots, visit our free resource websites below.

Visit **abdocorelibrary.com** for free Common Core resources for teachers and students, including vetted activities, multimedia, and booklinks, for deeper subject comprehension.

Visit **abdobooklinks.com** for free additional online weblinks for further learning. These links are routinely monitored and updated to provide the most current information available.

# LEARN MORE

Koontz, Robin. *Robotics in the Real World*. Minneapolis, MN: Abdo Publishing, 2016.

Otfinoski, Steven. *Making Robots*. New York: Scholastic, 2016.

# INDEX

## About the Author

George Anthony Kulz holds a master's degree in computer engineering. He is a member of the Society of Children's Book Writers and Illustrators and writes stories and nonfiction for children and adults. He currently lives in Rhode Island with his wife and four children.